POCKET BATTLESHIP
'ADMIRAL GRAF SPEE"

Siegfried Breyer

Schiffer Publishing Ltd

1469 Morstein Road, West Chester, Pennsylvania 19380

BIBLIOGRAPHY (Selected)

Bekker: Kampf und Untergang der Kriegsmarine, Hannover 1953.
Bekker, Radar: Duell im Dunkel, Oldenburg 1958.
Bekker: Die versunkene Flotte, Oldenburg 1961.
Bidlingmaier, Einsatz der Schweren Kriegsmarine-Einheiten im ozeanischen Zufuhrkrieg, Neckargemünd 1963.
Breyer, Schlachtschiffe und Schlachtkreuzer 1905-1970, Munich 1970.
Breyer/Koop, Von der EMDEN zur TIRPITZ, Munich 1980.
Gröner, Die deutschen Kriegsschiffe 1815-1945, Vol. 1, Munich 1982.
Hadeler, Kriegsschiffbau, Darmstadt, 1968.
Hildebrand/Röhr, Die deutschen Kriegsschiffe, Vol. 1, Herford 1969.
Rasenack, Panzerschiff ADMIRAL GRAF SPEE, Biberach 1957.
Rohwer/Hümmelchen, Chronik des Seekrieges 1939-1945, Oldenburg 1968.
Ruge, Der Seekrieg 1939-1945, Stuttgart 1954.

PHOTO CREDITS

Koop Collection: 19; Breyer Collection: 23; Library for History of the Times: 2; Scherl: 2; Weber: 4; Dressler Collection: 4; OKM: 2; Federal Archives: 1; Le Nasson: 2; DCN: 2; Schäfer: 3; "Ships of the World": 1.
   Drawings on pp. 8-9: official.
   All other drawings: Copyright S. Breyer
Cover picture: H. Helmus

Translated from the German by Dr. Edward Force.

Copyright © 1989 by Schiffer Publishing Ltd.
Library of Congress Catalog Number: 89-084177.

Printed in the United States of America.
ISBN: 0-88740-183-X

CONSTRUCTION HISTORY

The origin of the pocket battleship **ADMIRAL GRAF SPEE** goes back to the Weimar Republic era. After the **DEUTSCHLAND** and the **ADMIRAL SCHEER**, it was the third of its type, and likewise the last. Its building orders were still open in mid-1932. According to the naval command's plans, the ship was to be begun on October 1, 1932. At this time the navy wavered between the restrictions on naval construction set by the Treaty of Versailles, and a vague hope for equal rights soon and thus a release from the Versailles limitations. In the event that "compelling political reasons" would prevent the building of the third pocket battleship, a 6000-ton cruiser was to be contracted for, after the construction of four destroyers had first been discussed.

At this time the navy was already thinking in terms of a larger ship: it was to displace 15,000 to 18,000 tons and be armed with nine 28-cm guns. There were alternative suggestions to continue the construction of the pocket battleships, but to arm them with eight 20.3-cm guns, so as to make them "Washington cruisers" or heavy cruisers. Meanwhile Admiral Raeder, Chief of the naval command, decided that—if

on October 1, 1932 it was not a matter of taking liberties opposed to the Treaty of Versailles—the third pocket battle ship should be ordered built, and shortly afterward he announced that no objections would be raised "against an increase in displacement for the benefit of militarily important components". It happened exactly that way. On August 23, 1932 the Wilhelmshaven Naval Shipyard received the orders to build pocket battleship "C", which was booked under number 124. This was planned as a replacement for the obsolete liner **BRAUNSCHWEIG**, which had been built between 1901 and 1904, and had been crossed off the navy's list of warships on January 31, 1931 because it was too old, and after being used for a time as a hulk, was broken up.

View of the Wilhelmshaven Naval Shipyard, about mid-1933. In the background is Slipway I with the scaffolding around the growing pocket battleship C.

Diagonally in front—just visible at the right edge of the picture—is the light cruiser LEIPZIG, put in service in 1931.

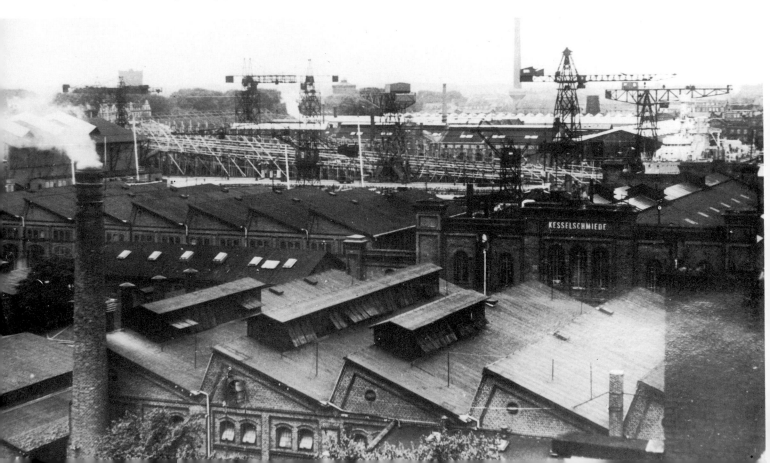

June 30, 1934: The pocket battleship, still at the christening pulpit; its name has just become visible after the name transparencies on either side have been unrolled.

The christened ship has been set in motion and glides more and more quickly into its element. At the left edge of the photo can be seen Slipway II, on which pocket battleship C had been begun. Because this slipway was to be used for the considerably enlarged pocket battleship D, the keel of which was laid in February of 1934 (work on which was nonetheless halted a few months later in favor of an even larger ship—the later SCHARNHORST), the already assembled or prepared steel components had to be moved to Slipway I beside it, which led to some delays. The scaffolding for pocket battleship D can be seen clearly here; only five days after this picture was taken, work on pocket battleship D was halted.

Before the keel was laid on October 1, 1932 on Slipway I of the Wilhelmshaven Naval Shipyard, part of the shipbuilding materials were put in readiness on the parallel Slipway II and partially assembled. These components were then moved to Slipway I by crane, after the second pocket battleship, ADMIRAL SCHEER, had been launched from it on April 1, 1933. This measure turned out to be necessary because Slipway II was needed for a larger ship—namely the enlarged pocket battleship D (which later became the battleship SCHARNHORST).

The launching of pocket battleship C took place 23 months after the keel was laid, on June 30, 1934. The christening address was given by Admiral Raeder as Chief of the Naval Command. Invited to christen the ship was Countess Huberta von Spee, the daughter of Vice-Admiral Count von Spee, who died in the sea battle of the Falkland Islands on December 8, 1914; she christened the ship with the name ADMIRAL GRAF SPEE. Nineteen months after that, on January 6, 1936, the ship was put in service. Thus the building time added up to 42 months, or three and a half years.

The launching again, taken from a somewhat more acute angle. At right in the background is the harbor canal which connected the shipyard harbor with the naval harbor (and still exists today).

ADMIRAL GRAF SPEE in the summer of 1934, shortly after the beginning of arming work. In the background at left is the old cruiser MEDUSA.

ADMIRAL GRAF SPEE at Kiel in 1937 for installation of the tenders. The port crane is just setting one on the grid, in order to pick up the tender still in the water.

MILITARY-TECHNICAL DETAILS

Compared to its forerunners DEUTSCH-LAND (later renamed LÜTZOW) and ADMIRAL SCHEER[1], the ADMIRAL GRAF SPEE, with otherwise almost equal outer dimensions[2], had an increase in the standard displacement of 1740 and 790 tons respectively. This increase, characterized by Admiral Raeder in 1932 as "expanded displacement", is essentially—as indicated by him—a matter of strengthening the durability, the defensive characteristics. For reasons of weight, in the first two ships the extension of the armored deck over the citadel, bordered by it and the two rampart bulkheads, had to be eliminated. Thanks to the strictly maintained secret of the ADMIRAL GRAF SPEE's increased displacement, the armored deck could be extended out over the entire width of the ship. In addition, it was also possible to extend the rampart bulkheads—which were to fulfill the function of torpedo bulkheads—to the keel. On the two previous ships they had reached only to the inner bottom. Likewise the armored transverse bulkheads and the foretops could be strengthened.

Armor

In the area of the citadel: upper area 80 mm, lower 50 mm, forward 17 mm, aft 18 mm. Armored transverse bulkheads: forward and aft each 100 mm. Splinter longitudinal bulkheads 40 mm. Rampart bulkheads 40 mm. Horizontal protection: Upper deck 17 mm, armored deck in the interior of the ship 20 mm, between splinter and rampart bulkheads 40 mm, between rampart bulkheads and hull 30 mm. Armor protection in the area of the rudder machinery: sides 40 mm, roof 45 mm, closing bulkhead 45 mm. Front command post: sides 150 mm, roof 50 mm, shaft 60 mm; aft command post: sides 50 mm. Foretop: 60 mm, roof 20 mm. 28-cm turrets: front 140 mm, sides 75-85 mm, roof 90-105 mm, rear side 170 mm, barbettes 125 mm; 15-cm guns: shields 10 mm.

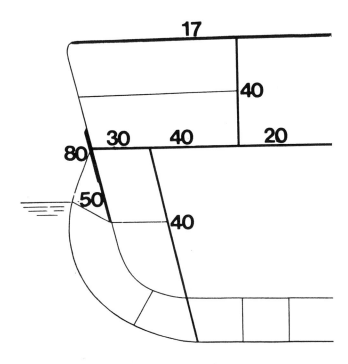

Schematic cut through the main rib surface. The numbers indicate the thickness of the armor in millimeters.

1) An edition of "Marine Arsenal" covering the ADMIRAL SCHEER will presumably be published in 1990.
2) Compared to the sister ship DEUTSCHLAND, the side height of the ADMIRAL SCHEER and ADMIRAL GRAF SPEE was 0.2 meters less.

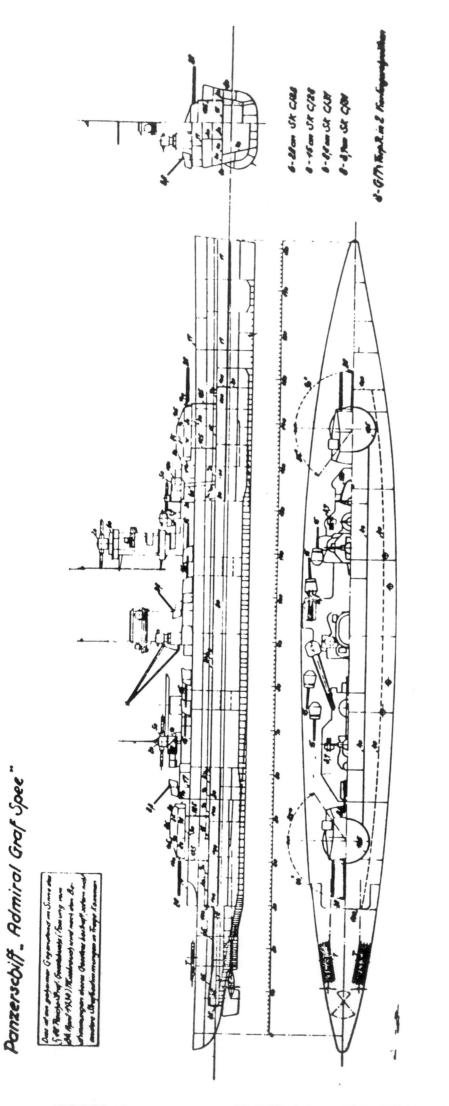

Panzerschiff „Admiral Graf Spee"

8

From the Planning Office of the Upper Command of the Navy: the type sketch of the third German pocket battleship.

Powerplant

Power was produced by a two-shaft-motor powerplant. Each shaft had, after construction, a power of 6750 HP; it was powered via vulcanized clutches by four fast-running double-action MAN two-stroke Diesel engines of type M-9 Z 42/58 (9 cylinders, each of 420 mm bore and 580 mm stroke, primary speed 450 rpm); all in all, there were thus eight motor units, each of 6750 HP, to provide a total power of 54,000 HP. The area was divided by transverse bulkheads into six chambers with four engine rooms and two drive rooms. In each engine room there was, along with the other auxiliary machinery, a 5-cylinder auxiliary diesel of type M-5 Z with the same characteristics as the main engines. The speed at which they were built to run was 26 knots; a speed of 28.5 knots was attained. At the end of each shaft was a three-bladed propeller of 4.40-meter diameter. The energy needed to run all the systems, weapons etc. was generated by eight Diesel generators with 3360 kw/220 volts in four units (two in each). Steering was done by a spade rudder of 49-square-meter rudder surface.

In the dock; view of the starboard shaft with the propeller.

Schematic drawing of the arrangement of the powerplant:

1. Main motor
2. Vulcanized clutch
3. Reduction gears
4. Thrust bearing
5. Blower motor
6. Flushing air fan
7. Fresh-water cooler
8. Lubricating oil filter
9. Diesel generator
10. Port shaft
11. Starboard shaft
12. Shaft tunnel
13. Tube passage
14. 15 cm shell and powder magazine

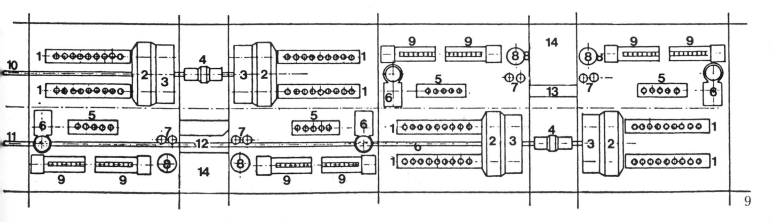

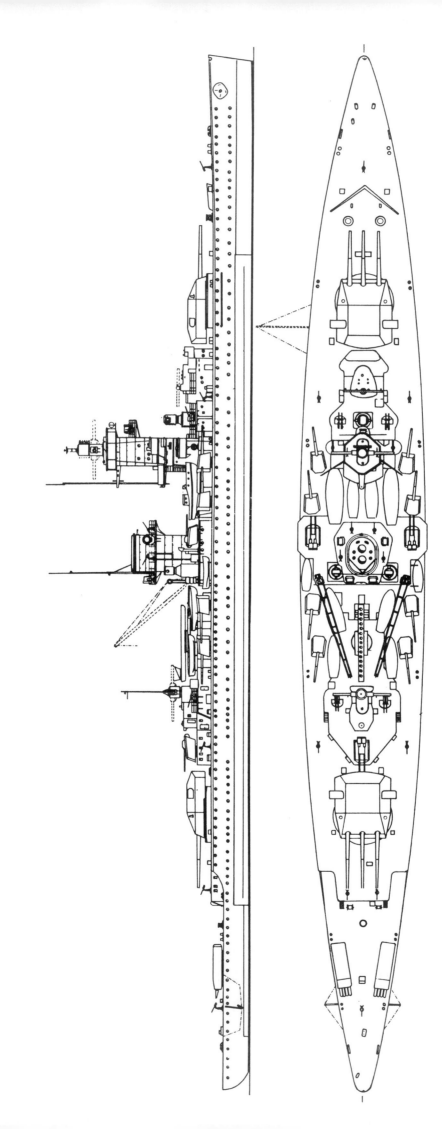

Side and top drawings of the armaments, as of summer 1939.

Armament

The armament essentially corresponded to that of the DEUTSCHLAND (see Marine Arsenal No. 6: Pocket Battleship DEUTSCHLAND/heavy cruiser LUTZOW). It consisted of:

1. Heavy artillery (SA): six 28-cm quick-loading cannon, L/52 C/28, on C 28 rotating mantlets within two triplet turrets with positions at the ends of the ship (ammunition supply: in all 630 to 720 rounds).

2. Medium artillery (MA): Eight 15-cm quick-loading cannon, L/55 C/28, on C 28 centrally pivoting mantlets (MPL) in single positions on the ship's sides (ammunition supply: in all 800 to 1000 rounds).

3. Heavy anti-aircraft guns, consisting of six 10.5-cm quick-loading cannon, L/65 C/33, in pairs on C 31 rotating mantlets (ammunition supply: 2400 to 3000 rounds).

4. Light anti-aircraft guns, consisting of eight 3.7-cm machine guns, L/83 C/30, on twin mantlets, with, in all, an ammunition supply of 8000 to 24,000 rounds.

5. Anti-aircraft machine guns, consisting of twelve 2-cm L/65 machine guns on C/30 socket mantlets, each with an ammunition supply of 2000 rounds.

6. Torpedo armament, consisting of eight tubes in groups of four, for 53.3-cm G 7 A torpedos.

Fire Control

The heavy artillery received their firepower from two 10.5-cm electric units in rotating cowlings; two additional 10.5-cm units were in the two heavy turrets as reserves. The power for the medium artillery was supplied by a 7-cm electric unit on the roof of the forward command post. For the heavy anti-aircraft guns there was—differing from the DEUTSCHLAND, which was still equipped only with two self-stabilizing SL-2 devices—a technical advance to the extent that the ADMIRAL GRAF SPEE used the improved, likewise self-stabilizing SL-4 device, of which three units— one for each pair of 10.5-cm anti-aircraft guns— were installed.

In 1938—at first on a trial basis—a "mattress" was installed on the foretop rotating cowling; that was the slang term for the antenna units of the then very new radar navigation system (for reasons of secrecy this "mattress" was covered with sailcloth in harbor). It was a prototype of the so-called FuMG 39 (gO). The outside dimensions of the antenna unit were: length 1.80 meters, height 0.8 meters.

For target illumination there were at first six triaxially stabilized, centrally controlled spotlights (four on the funnel platform circle and two on the turret mast); in 1938—along with the installation of the radar device—one of the turret mast spotlights was eliminated and the remaining one was moved.

In Kiel Harbor, 1938: at left ADMIRAL GRAF SPEE, in the background the new battleship GNEISENAU.

The On-board Aircraft Apparatus

Behind the funnel was a 14-meter aircraft catapult, as had been installed on the **DEUTSCHLAND** in 1935 and from the beginning on the **ADMIRAL SCHEER**. This gave the on-board aircraft—a He 60—its starting acceleration on a twelve-meter course. A second He 60 could be stored as a reserve if dismantled. In 1939 the He 60 was replaced by the newly introduced Ar-196. This gave excellent service during the war in the Atlantic, but its motor broke down during landing on December 11, 1939, resulting in a total loss. To handle both the on-board aircraft and the heavy tenders there were two cranes; these were located at either side behind the funnel. On the port side there was a landing sail, which could be swung out on a spar, below the turret mast. But this was eliminated in 1939; it was thrown overboard shortly after the war began, because it had proved to be more bother than it was worth.

ADMIRAL GRAF SPEE in Kiel Harbor, about 1938. Port spar and rope ladder are deployed, and tenders have made fast to them.

Statistical Data[1]

Building cost:	million Reichsmark	82
Standard displacement:	nautical tons	13,377[2]
Construction displacement:	tons	14,267
Full displacement:	tons	16,230
Dimensions:	BRT/NRT	9956/6299
Overall length:	meters	186.00
Length at construction waterline:	meters	181.70
Maximum width:	meters	21.65
Width at construction waterline:	meters	21.34
Depth by construction displacement:	meters	5.80
Depth at full displacement:	meters	7.34
Side height:	meters	12.20
Fuel oil supply, maximum:	tons	2749
Range:	nautical miles/ knots	8900/20
Peacetime crew:	men	951
Wartime crew:	men	1188

1) Essentially from data in the Koop collection, partially completed from Gröner, "Die deutschen Kriegsschiffe 1815-1945", Volume 1.

2) Until the war's end in 1945, the water displacement was always officially stated as 10,000 tons; this was also true of the two sister ships.

WEIGHT CATEGORIES (in tons) [1]

Body of the ship, including borne armor	3984
Armor (minus turrets)	2824
Main machine system	1678
Auxiliary machines	760
Artillery	2042
Torpedo system	60
On-board aircraft system	20
Weapon-locking system	6
General equipment	200
Nautical instruments	10
Ballast in stabilizing cells	164
Tackle	10
Empty Ship	**11758**
Ammunition: Artillery	562
Torpedos	21
Locking weapons	1
Consumed substances	25
Crew	99
Effects	70
Provisions	40
Standard displacement	12576
in nautical tons	12777
Drinking water	91
Washing water	110
Cooking water	36
Heating oil	78
Fuel oil	1285
Lubricating oil	83
Aircraft fuel	8
Construction displacement	14267
Cooking water	10
Heating oil	10
Fuel oil	1464
Lubricating oil	286
Fresh water reserve	253
Full displacement	16320

1) According to Hadeler, "Kriegsschiffbau", completed by data in the Koop collection.

Pocket battleship ADMIRAL GRAF SPEE on February 22, 1936 on the icy Jade, returning from a test cruise. The ice buildup on the bow occurs at that time of year.

The midsection of the ship with the 15-cm port battery. On the catapult is the He-60 on-board aircraft.

May 1936 in Kiel Harbor: Hitler pays a visit to the ADMIRAL GRAF SPEE (he can be seen standing with then-Admiral Raeder on the afterdeck of the tender that has just come alongside). The crew has come on deck; the commandant awaits the guests at the gangway. One deck higher—parallel to the aft 28-cm triplet turret—an honor guard presents arms.

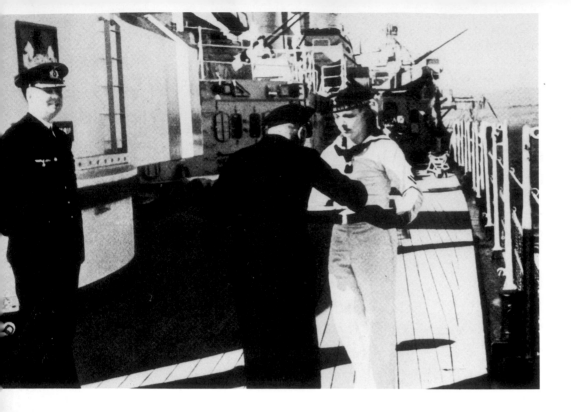

On the port deck at the level of "Bruno" turret: the Commander takes a food test. The picture was taken in 1937; at this time Sea Captain Warzecha commanded the ship.

From May 1936 on, **ADMIRAL GRAF SPEE** served as flagship of the fleet. Part of the fleet command on board was a navy band, which is giving a sample of its talents while standing under the gun barrels of "Bruno" turret.

Washing and painting are part of on-board routine on every warship—to this day. Here crew members on boatswain's chairs wash down the paintwork on the port bow.

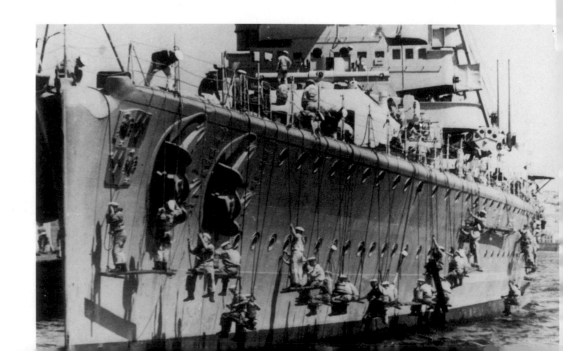

16

ADMIRAL GRAF SPEE seen from aft. The pocket battleship lies at a mooring buoy in Kiel Harbor, obviously during individual training. In the opposed light, the side armor is easy to see.

In June of 1937, ADMIRAL GRAF SPEE took part in the traditional naval review off Spithead held on the occasion of the coronation of George VI as King of Great Britain. This picture shows the crew on the upper deck giving a salute of honor.

The fleet in Kiel Harbor. This picture was taken in May of 1936 at the dedication of the Laboe naval monument. The pocket battleships, all flags flying, lie at mooring buoys—ADMIRAL GRAF SPEE in front, then ADMIRAL SCHEER and DEUTSCHLAND. Far in the background are light cruisers.

On special occasions German warships were seen in their ports with festive lighting. Here is the pocket battleship ADMIRAL GRAF SPEE in Kiel Harbor, probably in May of 1936.

Another view of the coronation naval review in Spithead roadstead, taken on May 20, 1937. In front is the pocket battleship ADMIRAL GRAF SPEE, behind it the British battleship RESOLUTION, and behind it the HOOD, pride of the Royal Navy and at that time the largest warship in the world. Four years later, almost to the day, the HOOD sank under fire from the BISMARCK.

ADMIRAL GRAF SPEE at anchor. The flags are at half-mast; the reason is not known. The British battleship of the RESOLUTION class visible in the left background suggests that the picture was taken in May of 1937 at Spithead roadstead. From there the pocket battleship began her return trip on May 22, 1937. (One week later there occurred the illegal attack on the pocket battleship DEUTSCHLAND before Ibiza by republican aircraft, which resulted in considerable loss of life. But this cannot be the reason for the mourning flags if the picture, as presumed, actually was taken at Spithead).

ADMIRAL GRAF SPEE at the Blücher Bridge in Kiel. The stern anchor, carried only on the port side, is easy to see. The emblem around the stern (on the bridge of smaller craft) was introduced after the National Socialists came to power.

19

In Kiel Harbor: ADMIRAL GRAF SPEE (with the fleet commander's flag at the foretop) and ADMIRAL SCHEER. Far in the background the despatch boat GRILLE can be seen.

Rest for the hardworking crew during service in Spanish waters. This picture is taken from the turret mast and shows the forward port side of the ship. A visible sign of the German warships in service off Spain is the black-white-red painted stripes on the heavy artillery turrets.

ADMIRAL GRAF SPEE makes the run to see service off Spain. Here crew members are stowing the piles of provisions and other supplies stacked on the afterdeck; these had been taken aboard in great haste in Wilhelmshaven. An empty wooden crate is just being thrown overboard, as there is no more room for it on board.

ADMIRAL GRAF SPEE in the Atlantic in April of 1939, where extended maneuvers took place. This picture was taken from the destroyer FRIEDRICH IHN.

In the inner fjord at Kiel: the Type II-B submarine U 14 passes the anchored ADMIRAL GRAF SPEE.

ADMIRAL GRAF SPEE, about 1938, passing the high bridge at Levensau on the Kiel Canal.

On June 19, 1938, anchored at Wilhelmshaven roadstead. A few days later the pocket battleship began a training voyage to Norway.

ADMIRAL GRAF SPEE in the Hipper Harbor at Wilhelmshaven, lying at the Seydlitz Pier.

In the summer of 1939 the pocket battleship's crew were able to enjoy the beauty of the Norwegian fjord region during a training voyage.

In the latter half of 1938, various changes were made to the mast tower of the pocket battleship ADMIRAL GRAF SPEE. The most visible mark of this was the new spotlight platform mounted on the front of the mast tower; the former positions at the same height on either side had had to be removed.

During an Atlantic training voyage in the spring of 1939, ADMIRAL GRAF SPEE put in at the port of Ceuta in Spanish Morocco. This photo was taken from on board the ALTMARK (which operated along with the ADMIRAL GRAF SPEE several months later) and shows the pocket battleship with the submarine tender ERWIN WASSNER moored behind her, and several submarines.

The landing sail carried on the port side—it is easy to see between the mast tower and the smokestack below—was dismantled soon after the war began and, as there was nothing else to do, thrown overboard in the operation zone. It had proved to be unhandy, and in addition, another method had meanwhile been put into practice that made possible a simpler and less risky way to lift the aircraft on board, the so-called "duck pond".

Change of the fleet commander in the fall of 1938: According to an old tradition, the former commander of the fleet, Admiral Carls, is taken off in a cutter manned by young officers (his successor is Admiral Boehm). For this occasion, the crews of the warships lying in Kiel took parade position. Here the cutter with Admiral Carls on board (standing and saluting) has just put off from the ADMIRAL GRAF SPEE; soon the command to let the oars fall will be heard. Although the new battleship GNEISENAU had fulfilled the function of flagship for the fleet since August of 1938, this honor, because of her longer time in shipyard, was temporarily given back to the ADMIRAL GRAF SPEE.

ADMIRAL GRAF SPEE as seen from an aircraft, taken in the spring of 1939. The muffled radar antenna on the rotating foretop cowling is easy to see. Photos in which this antenna could be seen in uncovered condition were not released by the supreme command of the navy for reasons of secrecy.

Maintaining tradition had a very high priority in the German Navy—as in every other navy. Not only did turrets bear the names of well-known personalities and scenes of action, but so did certain other structures. On ADMIRAL GRAF SPEE the front side of the mast tower bore a plaque with the inscription "Coronel". This recalled the victorious battle of the cruiser squadron led by Vice-Admiral Count von Spee against a British cruiser group off Coronel (south of Valparaiso, Chile) on November 1, 1914.

View forward from the starboard side deck. At left front is the after 10-meter electric unit's rotating cowling with the after antenna mast, which simultaneously served as a flagpole. The catapult can be seen just in front of it. In the background is the funnel with the circular platform for spotlights and anti-aircraft machine guns, typical of large German warships at that time. Also typical of German "big ships" was the large mast erected right by the funnel.

ADMIRAL GRAF SPEE in Atlantic swells, taken in the autumn of 1938. At such times the afterdeck, lying one deck below the main deck, proved not to be so good. In heavy after seas it could not be occupied, and equipment such as torpedo housings, fog buoys and such almost always went overboard. This

disadvantage was to be eliminated in the process of rebuilding all three pocket battleships, but that never took place. The main purpose of this rebuilding was the desire to increase the speed to 29 or 30 knots, for which new motors were to be installed.

Spring 1939: ADMIRAL GRAF SPEE on its last peacetime training voyage, here with a Mediterranean landscape in the background.

LIFE STORY IN BRIEF

1/6/1936	Put in service at Wilhelmshaven (Commander: Sea Captain Patzig.
5/9/1936	After release from test status, joined the fleet; since then fleet flagship (until August 1938).
5/29/1936	Fleet parade in Kiel Bay on occasion of naval monument dedication in Laboe.
6/6-26/1936	Test voyage in the Atlantic, making port at Santa Cruz, Canary Islands.
8/20-10/9/1936	Service in Spanish waters because of Spanish Civil War.
12/13/1936- 2/14/1937	Second service in Spanish waters.
3/2-5/22/1937	Third service in Spanish waters.
5/15-22/1937	Participation in international naval review at Spithead Roadstead on occasion of coronation of King George VI.
6/23-8/7/1937	Fourth service in Spanish waters.
9/18-20/1937	After participation in yearly fleet maneuvers, visit to Visby, Sweden.
10/1/1937	Change of command. New commander is Sea Captain Warzecha.

12/1-2/1937	Visit to Kristiansand, Norway.
6/29-7/9/1938	Training cruise to Norway.
8/22/1938	Participation in fleet parade in Kiel Bay on the occasion of the state visit of the Hungarian regent, Admiral von Horthy.
10/1/1938	Change of command. New commander is Sea Captain Langsdorff.
10/6-23/1938	Atlantic training voyage, making port at Vigo and Tangier.
11/10-24/1938	Atlantic training voyage, making port in Portugal at Bilbao.
3/22-24/1939	Participation in the absorption of the Memel area into Germany.
4/18-5/16/1939	Atlantic training voyage along with pocket battleships DEUTSCHLAND and ADMIRAL SCHEER, cruisers LEIPZIG and KOLN, destroyer DIETMAR VON ROEDER, submarine tender DIETHER VON ROEDER, and submarine flotillas "Salzwedel", "Hundius" and "Wegener", making port at Ceuta and Lisbon.
5/29-31/1939	Honor escort for the "Condor Legion" returning on KdF ships from Spain to Hamburg.
8/21/1939	Departed Wilhelmshaven for the South Atlantic.
9/1/1939	War begins.

WAR DIARY

September 1939 After leaving Wilhelmshaven on August 21, held a waiting position in remote sea area some 900 sea miles east of Bahia from September 11 to 25. Was cleared for operations on September 26. First target, the British freighter CLEMENT (5051 BRT) stopped and sunk off Pernambuco on September 30.

October 1939 On the steamship lane Capetown-Freetown: On October 5 the British freighter NEWTON BEACH (4651 BRT), on October 7 the British freighter ASHLEA (4222 BRT), on October 10 the British freighter HUNTSMAN (8196 BRT), and on October 22 the British motor ship TREVANION (5299 BRT) were stopped. NEWTON BEACH and HUNTSMAN were occupied by prize crews and sunk only on October 8 and 17, the other ships were sunk at once.

November 1939 Advance into the Indian Ocean from November 4 to 19, sinking the British motor tanker AFRICA SHELL (706 BRT) on November 15.

December 1939 After return to previous operation zone, following sinkings: On December 2 the British freight steamer DORIC STAR (10086 BRT) and on December 3 the British refrigerator ship TAIROA (7983 BRT). At 25.5 degrees south, 24.5 degrees west its last rendezvous with the supply ship ALTMARK took place on December 6; in all, ADMIRAL GRAF SPEE had taken on fuel from the ALTMARK nine times (first time on September 1). To disguise intention of returning home, advanced southwest to La Plata; a course around Cape Horn into the Pacific was thus to be suggested.*) On December 7 the British freight steamer STREANSALH (3895 BRT) was stopped and sunk. On December 13, off the mouth of La Plata, met the cruiser pack of the British South American Squadron under command of Commodore Harwood, consisting of the heavy cruiser EXETER and the light cruisers AJAX and ACHILLES. ADMIRAL GRAF SPEE succeeded in putting EXETER out of action and damaging AJAX strongly and ACHILLES lightly. On the EXETER there are 61 dead and 23 wounded, on the AJAX 7 dead and 5 wounded, on the ACHILLES 4 dead. With 36 dead and 60 wounded, ADMIRAL GRAF SPEE had to run for Montevideo on account of her own damage. On December 17 the pocket battleship was destroyed because repair was impossible within the time allowed by the Uruguayan government. The commander, Sea Captain Langsdorff, committed suicide on December 20.

---

*) According to the naval commander's report to Hitler on November 1, 1939, ADMIRAL GRAF SPEE had announced its breakthrough and return to Germany in January 1940, in order to carry out, among other things, the engine overhaul long intended but postponed because of the threat of war.

The mast tower seen from the side. The shorter upper part of the topmast on its back could be retracted by a hand crank in the longer lower part, in order to pass under the bridges over the Kiel Canal. The forward port 3.7-cm double anti-aircraft guns are easy to see.

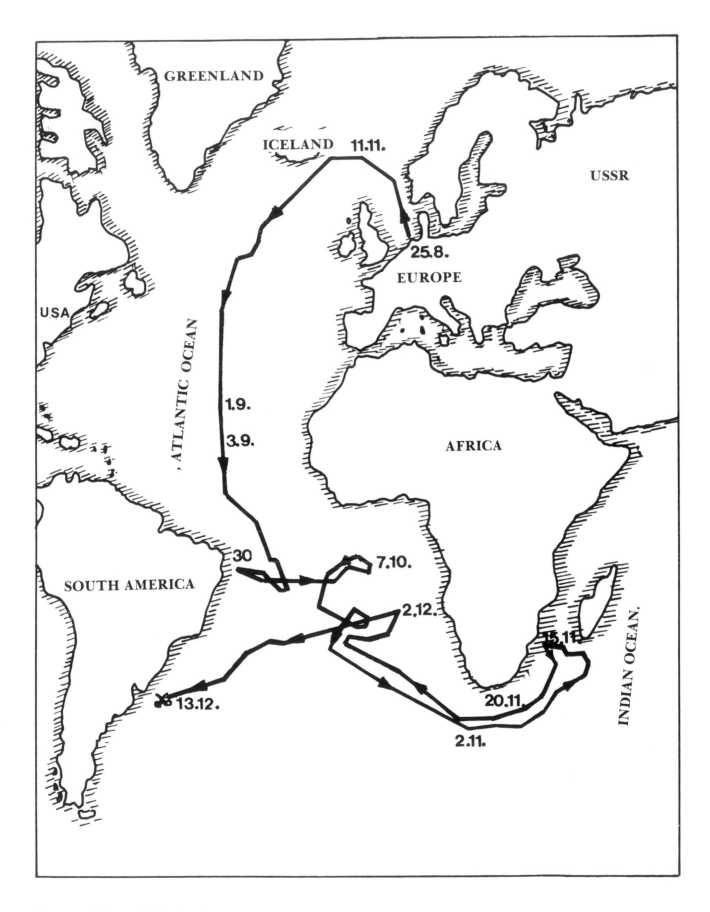

The route of the pocket battleship ADMIRAL GRAF SPEE. The dates show the ship's positions on those dates.

THE HUNTERS OF THE "SPEE"

At the beginning of October 1939, eight British and French battle groups were formed for action against the ADMIRAL GRAF SPEE in the South Atlantic. These consisted of three battleships, four aircraft carriers, ten heavy and three light cruisers in all—an impressive amount of superior power. The strongest unit in terms of artillery was the British RENOWN, a 32-knot, 32,000-ton battle cruiser with six 38.1-cm and twenty 11.4-cm guns.

Equally dangerous opponents: the 30-knot, 26,500-ton battleship STRASBOURG (photo) and its sister ship DUNKERQUE. Each had eight 33-cm and sixteen 13-cm guns. They belonged to the French Navy.

A relatively slow aircraft carrier was the French BE/ARN (21,800 tons, 40 aircraft): its top speed was only 21 knots.

The ARK ROYAL was the newest and most effective aircraft carrier in the Royal Navy. It had a displacement of 22,600 tons, a top speed of 30.7 knots, and could carry 60 aircraft.

The chief opponent in the encounter of December 13, 1939 at the mouth of La Plata was the British heavy cruiser EXETER (8390 tons, 32.2 knots, six 20.3-cm guns). It was knocked out of action and lost 61 crewmen.

The British light cruiser AJAX (6985 tons, 32.5 knots, eight 15.2-cm guns) and its sister ship ACHILLES were the other two opponents of the German pocket battleship. They too suffered damage and losses. The photo shows the AJAX.

During the operation, camouflage structures were used to change the silhouette and look to the enemy like a different ship. Here wood and sailcloth have been used, under orders from above, to erect a higher front turret and a second funnel. This photo from the tender ALTMARK shows the ADMIRAL GRAF SPEE in this state of mimicry. Added above is the new, intentionally confusing silhouette.

This is how ADMIRAL GRAF SPEE looked when it ran to Montevideo. The shell damage is easy to see.

Of the on-board Ar-196 aircraft (already out of commission before the December 13 battle), little remained but the ribs. Here too, the effects of shelling are readily visible on the hull.

ADMIRAL GRAF SPEE after the scuttling explosion. The view goes from the bow toward the bridge-mast tower area.

A view from the mast tower to the front of the bridge with the battle command post in the foreground; behind it is the front 28-cm turret.

Also seen from the mast tower: the funnel tipping to starboard from the force of the explosion. Around it is the platform crane with spotlights and anti-aircraft guns.

The 10.5-cm double anti-aircraft gun on the port side after the explosion.

This is how ADMIRAL GRAF SPEE looked after the explosion was set off. She sank in shallow water and lay in this position for four years.

It took three days and nights before the fires were extinguished—of the pocket battleship there remained only a thoroughly borned-out wreck. Her entire crew had been taken to Buenos Aires on tugboats shortly before the explosion; they were interned there, and could return home only after the war ended.

The commander, Sea Captain Langsdorff, shot himself during the night of December 20, to die "for the honor of the flag". His last resting place is in Buenos Aires.

CURRENT NAVAL INFORMATION

Charles de Gaulle:
France's First Nuclear Aircraft Carrier

France's carrier force consists of two 32,700-ton, conventionally powered aircraft carriers, each with approximately 40 airplanes and helicopters on board. Their names are **CLEMENCEAU** and **FOCH**. They have been in service for more than a quarter century and have come very close to obsolescence by now. This will in the forseeable future make their retirement necessary for economic reasons alone. Thus the question of replacing them moved to a new stage. The first considerations in this direction already took place in the mid-Seventies: plans came into being on the drawing board for a helicopter carrier displacing barely 15,000 tons but nuclear powered, with the alternative of carrying up to 25 "Lynx" helicopters or an adequate assortment of various helicopters. This project, carried on under the name "PA 74/75, was finally rejected on the basis of test results showing that it was more appropriate to take up the replacement of the two existing carriers as soon as possible and work on ships of similar size. These considerations led in the autumn of 1980 to a decision by the appropriate government board; it was decided to replace the carriers **CLEMENCEAU** and **FOCH**, to be retired in or after 1996, with appropriate new ships, both of which should be nuclear-powered. The first of these, **CHARLES DE GAULLE**, had its keel laid during 1989. It is being built at the naval shipyard in Brest. The launch is to take place in 1992, and the ship is to be put in service in 1996. At this time the **CLEMENCEAU** is to be retired—she will have served for 35 years by then, more than any other comparable ship of the French Navy. The second nuclear-powered carrier—it will provisionally be named **RICHELIEU**—will be started later; it will replace the **FOCH**, then 38 years old, whose retirement is planned for the year 2001.

The atomic-powered aircraft carrier CHARLES DE GAULLE in figures

Type/action displacement	tons	34,000/36,000
Overall/KWL*) length	meters	261.50/238.00
Width at flight deck/KWL*)	meters	64.36/31.50
Depth at type displacement	meters	8.45
Reactors		2 150-MW Type K-15 heavywater reactors
Powerplant		2 steam turbines with gearing
Power, WPS	(kw)	82,000 (60,338)
Shafts/propellers		2/2 (5-bladed)
Top speedknots		27-28
Electric system		10 turbodynamos (4x2000 kW & 6x850 kW, total 13,100 kW
Crew		1700 (including 500 flight & air-technical personnel.)

*) KWL = construction waterline

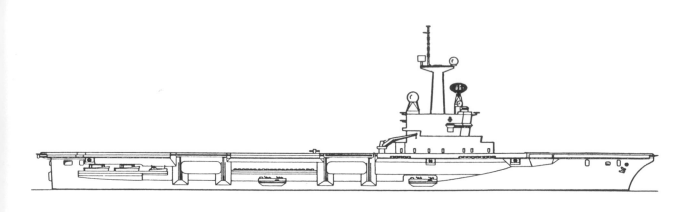

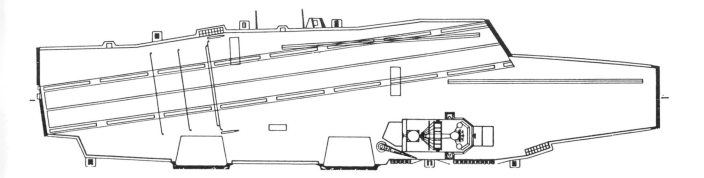

FLIGHT DECK

Flight deck dimensions	Length 261.5 meters, width to 64.36 m, surface 12,300 sq.m. (angled deck area length 195 m, running at 8.3-degree angle to port from ship's axis).
Hangar deck dimensions	Length 138 m, width 29.0 m, height 6.1 m
Aircraft elevators	2 outside elevators (length 19 m, width 12.5 m, lifting power 40 tons)
Catapults	2 steam catapults, each 75 m long (American C 13 F system)
Aircraft	35-40, including "Super-Etendard" (to be replaced by new type in 1999)
Aircraft fuel supply	3000 cubic meters
Defensive armament	1 ship-to-air-rocket weapons system in 8 under-deck vertical launchers, each with 7 rockets (total = 56 rockets), plus 3 6-part starters for "Sadral" close-range ship-to-air rockets, 4 20-mm antiaircraft guns

This shows how the aircraft carrier CHARLES DE GAULLE is to look when it is finished.

Another drawing showing how the new carrier will look.

China: Newest Member of SSBN "Club"

SSBN * , as sea-supported nuclear strategic components, hold an important position in the navies of the atomic powers. In addition to the USA and the Soviet Union, until now only Great Britain and France have possessed such SSBN. Now the People's Republic of China has entered this "club" as the fifth member: in 1985 its first SSBN made its debut. This and its identically built successor belong to the "Xia" class. "Xia" is not a Chinese designation, but the code name for this class used in the western world.

The development of the "Xia" class is obviously based on two "building blocks": One is a conventionally driven U-boat (SSB) that was built in the People's Republic of China according to plans for the Soviet "Golf-I" class; the plans and construction models were turned over to the People's Republic by the Soviets at a time when relations between the two were less strained. This boat was probably introduced mainly as a test platform for the strategic U-boat rockets developed in the People's Republic; the first U-boat rockets could be launched from it in October of 1982.

The development of nuclear propulsion systems had already been taken up in the Sixties, and led in 1974 to the introduction of the first SSN ** of the "Han" class. At large intervals of time, four units have been added, whereby improvements could be added step by step. With this class, the basis was obviously created on which the propulsion system for the "Xia" class could be developed.

Such knowledge as is available concerning the "Xia" class is still scant and may have only limited validity, to the extent of setting parameters. The displacement when underwater is estimated at 7000 to 8000 tons, and the external dimensions are thought to be about 120 meters in overall length, 10 meters in width and 8 meters of depth. Presumably it has a turbo-electric single-shaft powerplant, with a heavy-water reactor to provide heat. The underwater speed is probably 20 to 22 knots. As to armament, it is definite that it consists of twelve launching shafts (two rows of six each) for ballistic rockets of the CSS-NX 3 type. These rockets, powered by two-stage solid-fuel engines, carry a single nuclear warhead in the 2-megaton range and fly approximately 1500 sea miles (' 2780 km); they presumably find their target with the help of an inertia navigation system. Torpedo tubes may also be included.

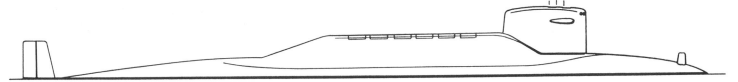

Side-view drawing of the "Xia" class (above) and the "Han" class (below).

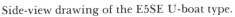

Side-view drawing of the E5SE U-boat type.

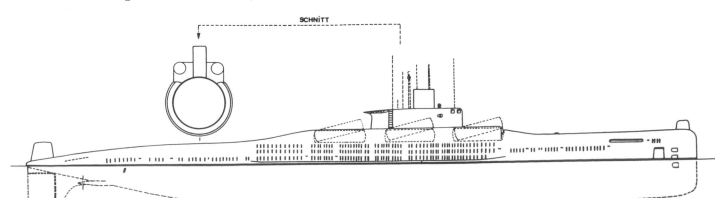

Nuclear strategic U-cruiser of the "Xia" class on the surface, as seen from the air.

The SSBN of the "Xia" class are built in the Huludao shipyard, probably opened in the Sixties in the northern part of the People's Republic. One or two units are in service; two others are being equipped. All in all, construction seems to drag along; it may be that construction is taken slowly on purpose because of still unsolved technical problems or unsatisfactory solutions, so as, perhaps, to be able to include further improvements. A total of four "Xia" can be expected to be ready for service by the mid-Nineties. The doubtless continually extended planning may meanwhile have reached a stage at which in the future a "full-value" type, with sixteen rockets, can be expected, for which a new rocket arming system with improved performance will probably be available.

The four SSBN of the "Han" class were also built in Huludao. This shipyard seems to be the first (and thus far only) shipbuilding works in the People's Republic of China that has the capacity to build U-boats. There is as yet no evidence that conventionally powered U-boats or surface vessels have also been built there. The following data are available for the "Han" class: displacement underwater 4500 to 5000 tons, outer dimensions: length 90-100 m, width 8-11 m, power: turboelectric single-shaft system with a heavy-water reactor to produce energy, speed: 25 knots underwater, 30 knots underwater. Armament consists of torpedos. Thus this class amounts to an "attack type" in essence. Whether more will be built is not known; from today's point of view, it looks unlikely. It is more likely that in the coming years a successor SSN type, more highly developed in technical terms, will appear.

Other Chinese activities aimed at making U-boat weapons more efficient are also noteworthy. The Soviet "Romeo" class, built for years under license (between 1960 and 1982 more than 100 units were built, some of which were passed on to North Korea and Egypt), was the source of the "Ming" class derived in the early Seventies (designated E5SE by the Chinese) and, building on this, a variant in the form of a carrier of tactical rocket weapons against ship and land targets (project designation E5SG). Without any great changes in construction, dimensions and degree of completion, a remarkable guided-missile-carrying version was created in an obviously very uncomplicated manner. On both sides of the tower, and before and abaft it, three individual launchers, erectable to 15 degrees, for C-801 rockets are installed; they can, to be sure, only be fired from the surface. These rockets—designated "Ying Ji" by the Chinese—are said to have "sea skimmer" capability. They have a range of 25 to 40 sea miles, are only 5.2 meters long and reach a wingspan of 1 meter; their flight speed is about Mach 0.9. Of a launch weight of about 1000 kg, the warhead is thought to account for 165 kg; it can, though, be armed only with a conventional load. This rocket finds its target with an integrated radar target-seeking head. Since these U-boats can also carry 18 torpedos or alternatively 28 mines on board, they rank as notably effective battle units despite the weak points of their conventional construction.

*) SSBN = Submarine Ballistic Missile Nuclear powered, including nuclear-powered U-cruisers with ballistic rockets for nuclear strategic warfare.
**) SSN = Submarine Nuclear powered, generally understood to mean a nuclear-powered U-boat for conventional submarine warfare, with torpedos and/or mines.

Another view of a U-cruiser of the "Xia" class.

Nuclear-powered attack submarine of the "Han" class.

Conventionally powered U-boat of Type E5SE firing a rocket.

New Rocket Destroyer for the U.S. Navy

Up to 29 new rocket destroyers are to be received by the U.S. Navy in the Nineties. This class, named ARLEIGH BURKE for the first ship, is intended to replace the destroyers of the COONTZ and CHARLES F. ADAMS classes, built in the late Fifties and the Sixties, the retirement of which cannot be delayed for long. In comparison to them, the ARLEIGH BURKE class will show a considerable increase in firepower, mainly because they will be equipped with the AEGIS SPY-1D system, a lighter version of the system installed on rocket cruisers of the TICONDEROGA class. With a size of 6624/8315 tons (standard/action displacement), these new vessels already correspond to the norms of cruisers. Their main dimensions also show this: length overall/at construction waterline 153.77/142.03 meters, width over deck/at construction waterline 20.4/18.0 meters, depth maximally/over bow sonar bulge 6.09/9.32 meters. Four General Electric LM 25-30 gas turbines with a total power of 100,000 horsepower (73,580 KW) will provide the power, two driving each of the two shafts fitted with five-bladed propellers. This should allow a speed of 30 knots and more. Available as armament are:

Two Mark 41 Model O underdeck vertical launchers of 64 cells (aft) or 32 cells (forward), with a payload of, in all, 90 "Standard SM-2 MR Block 4 ship-to-air "Asroc" sub-chasing and "Tomahawk" ship-to-ship rockets, individually positioned' eight "Harpoon" ship-to-ship rockets in two groups of four canisters;

one 127-mm Mark 45 Model 1 DP cannon;

two 20-mm Gatling Mark 15 CIWS anti-aircraft guns;

six 324-mm anti-submarine torpedo tubes.

An on-board helicopter is not planned, but there will be helicopter landing capability.

The launch of the first ship, the keel of which was laid in April of 1988, is planned for the summer of 1990.

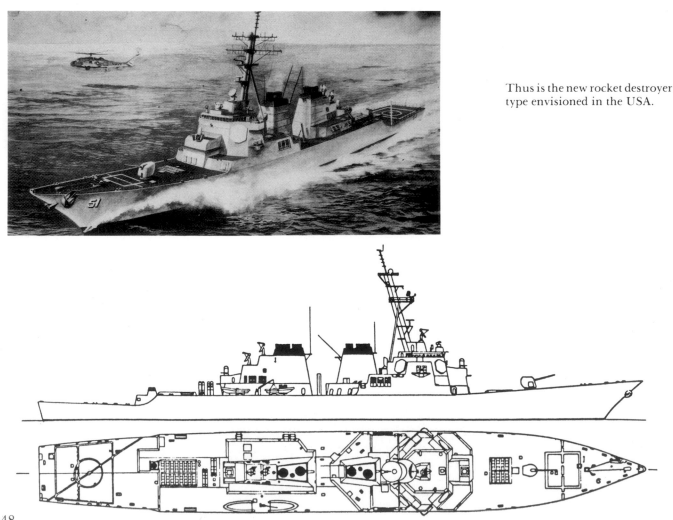

Thus is the new rocket destroyer type envisioned in the USA.